AF433785

Period of Calm:
Beyond The Storm

Hujefa Vohra

Writer's Pocket

First published by Writer's Pocket in 2023

email: publish@writerspocket.com

cover design by Rutuja Shelke

ISBN-13: 978-93-6083-372-5

www.writerspocket.com

Acknowledgments

You thought I would forget about you all but no, never, because you are the ones to BLAME for this book, you who put me through this intense form of exercise of writing the acknowledgement!

My friends and family that knowing-unknowingly told me to do something with my life.

My English Teachers, Joicy Ma'am and Sugandha Ma'am, where one introduced me to poetry and the other refined my skills.

My brothers Kunal & Harsh who spent an insane amount of time listening to Eminem and thought they too had a shot.

And finally, I Blame the friends, I made through Discord, who kept me awake when I just wanted to sleep!

And you the casual reader, you are to Blame if you did not buy this book!

1. Story of a Cloud

Dark and threatening, a certain times...
A shadow hiding the truth, the lies & crimes...
With such fierce and deafening roar...
Shattering me to my core...

But suddenly this violent beast starts to weep...
The anguish and burden, it cannot keep...
A rampageous rain and a scream so loud...
Is such the story of a cloud...?

2. Against No One

Against no one I shall kneel...
This pain, I won't reveal...
There's so much that I feel...
And these scars, they don't heal...

I will no longer let anyone hurt me...
I will No longer be the same...
I won't let myself be happy...
I will show you how to play this game...

3. Am I?

Am I not allowed to have a choice...?
Am I not allowed to speak my voice...?
Am I not allowed to shut this noise...?

Am I not allowed to be free...?
Am I not allowed to disagree...?
Am I not allowed to escape or to flee...?

Am I not allowed to heal or mend...?
Am I not allowed to be content...?
Am I not allowed to choose my end...?

Am I supposed to just follow...?
Am I supposed to feel so shallow...?
Am I supposed to be so hollow...?

Am I supposed to not shed a tear...?
Am I supposed to live with fear...?
Am I supposed to, disappear...?

Am I supposed to only make mistakes...?
Am I supposed to be the one that breaks...?
Am I supposed to drown in these aches...?

Am I nothing but a burden to all...?
Am I nothing but meant to fall...?
Am I nothing? I am nothing, I recall...!

Am I nothing but a product of your greed...?

Am I nothing even though I bleed...?
Am I nothing? I am nothing indeed...!

Am I nothing? Just an unheard cry...?
Am I nothing? I no longer try...!
Am I nothing? I am nothing, die...!

Am I destined to beg for your aid...?
Am I destined to play a charade...?
Am I destined, to fade...?

Am I destined to suffer this torment...?
Am I destined to your resent...?
Am I destined? To what extent...?

4. Battle Alone

Behind me an empty castle...
In front of me an army...
I stand strong in this battle...
No one shall harm me...
Fighting them all alone...
While my loved ones just stare...
Fighting with my crushed collarbone...
Thinking 'How much can I truly bare...?'

I looked at the blood on my sword...
And then gazed towards the sky...
Memorizing and thanking the lord...
As I say goodbye...

5.

Back into this battle with pain...
My own blood on my sword...
Nothing but only the dead remain...
I say 'Mercy, oh Lord!'...
I see nothing but the fallen...
All dragged to death...
My pride, it was stolen...
I wait for the end with my last breath...

6.

All that is lost, now comes before my eyes,
Give me strength, I want to rise.
But this time, he won't listen,
this world, it seems like a prison...
I can't escape alive... Only thing I see is death in front of
my eyes...
My friends and family I see...
I remember, I hurt 'em
While on my battle spree
Causing trouble, creating mayhem...
For all the pain I have caused...
Now I want to apologize...

Everything has paused...
While, I agonize...

7.

Two gates on either side...
Heaven and Hell's game...
I have sinned and I have lied...
'He should burn in the Eternal Flame'...

A gate opens, I walk inside...
Suddenly life and death are the same...
On every step I collide...
A burning man asks my name...

8.

Afterlife, I heard somewhere...
Torturous it would be...
My kills in front, I just stare...
I don't know what you want me to see...

Hell is nothing but despair...
Even the Devil would agree...
I could not be elsewhere...
Because the burning man is me...

9. Beautiful Chaos

Even this beautiful world is filled with chaos...
There's a certain limit, that none shall cross...
No one is an absolute diamond, everyone's got flaws...
When pushed off limits even a coward can use their
claws...

Maybe you weren't worth the fight...
Everything is falling apart in my sight...
Only tears in my eyes at night...
Will ever my day ever be bright...?

10. Black and White

The night used to be my friend...
The day, just to pretend...
The shadows that didn't haunt...
The shines I didn't want...

But now I fear the absence of light...
The hours of darkness in my sight...
The black and white that I cannot escape...
The right and wrong that I cannot reshape...

11. Broken Isn't Bad

Broken isn't bad...
Once you open your eyes...
Broken isn't bad...
Just a life full of lies...
Broken isn't bad...
What's bad is its ache...
Broken isn't bad...
It's the life that is fake...
Broken isn't bad...
It's a story to reveal...
Broken isn't bad...
If you have someone to heal...

12. Busy

I sit in peace; I see them pace away...
And I wonder...
They work all day and just obey...
Where's the thunder...?
Halt, breath, close your eyes once a day...
Before you begin...
Your entire life is the price you pay...
To be in the skin...

Until on death bed when the reaper slay...
And you feel your life fading away...
From within and under...

13. The Eye

Pain and sorrow as I look behind...
A lost soul, I still try to find...
Dare to turn towards the right...
A chilling sensation to which I fright...
Then took a step to the left...
Lost my sanity to its theft...
Shivering I walk ahead...
A thought of me, being dead...

A cold breeze up above...
And here am I deprived of love...
Ferocious flame down below...
And suddenly, the world is slow...

14. A New Start

Thanking the God for this new start...
No more pain or any regret...
Nothing can now break me apart...
I step forward, my past I forget...

15. Tears

Cried buckets of tears...
I am ashamed of myself...
I can't conquer my fears...
Just try to kill myself...

16. A King

Where I deserve from there, I was thrown...
With the passage of time, I've grown...
I've turned myself into an emotionless drone....
The king is back to reclaim his throne...

17. Despair

A reoccurring nightmare...
Trying to escape but,
Stuck in despair...

Shattering my pride...
I try to run with
Immense that I hide...

It is driving me insane...
But I can not
Cease this pain...

Peace is all I want...
But these fears,
They haunt...

Every blessing is a curse
Like a ceaseless pain,
Stuck in reverse...

18. Diminish

The inevitable truth is death...
The inevitable pain, our existence...
You lose time with every breath...
We all have the fear of evanescence...

Ourselves is who we betray...
When there is no scream or cry...
Cause at the end of the day...
We will diminish and die...

19. Dream

I'm only happy I imagine...
With no sadness around...
Could this be true, I think...
Or to sorrow I'm bound...

The peace I enjoy...
With the sound of this stream...
I open my eyes to destroy,
This unrivalled dream...

20. Drowned

Only in the presence of light,
Can you know it's black...
Succumb to the void in sight...
The will to survive, you lack...

Turn around in the blind...
Afraid to make a sound...
Adapt and free your mind...
Know, in the dark you are drowned...

21. Everything I Love

Everything I love just goes away...
I really thought that you would just stay...
The one you are proud will just fade...
Trust me dear soul, you'll get no aid...

My life's nothing more than a curse...
No market for our feelings to adverse...
Wish I could hit reverse...
Wish I could roam the whole universe...

22. Fear

I feel no fear...
Everything I lost...
I feel no fear...
My emotions are frost...
I feel no fear...
As I'm always alone...
I feel no fear...
There's no one I've known...
I feel no fear...
Emptiness instead...
I feel no fear...
Cause I'm nothing but dead...

23. For You

Fight with you till I cry...
Fight for you till I die...
Fight besides till I fall apart...
Just for you with all my heart...

Arrows shall stop mid-air...
Till I stand as your shield...
No pain that I cannot bare...
Cause with you I am healed...

24. Force

Force is a nice word....
It's free like a bird...
From there voices can be heard...
Step into it and the vision gets blurred...

What you call trust...
Is just another T with rust...
At the end we all are going into the earth's crust...
With living, death is a must...

25. Restless

From myself I'm falling helplessly...
Myself I'm killing endlessly....
To the hell gate I run breathlessly...
Can't understand whom I'm killing so recklessly...
Where's the devil, haven't waited for anyone this
restlessly...

26. Heart Heavy

When the heart weighs heavy...
And the thoughts get blurry...
I keep my hands steady...
As I drown and I worry...

When the legs go numb...
And the body feels dead...
To fear and madness I succumb...
'Till my soul is fed...

My eyes fixated; it is the right time...
To write what I feel and try to rhyme...

27. Hurt

I swear I thought that you'd react...
But you didn't, you don't care maybe that's the fact...
But you did care for me that's something I've seen...
This is the worst from which I've been...
Look what have you done...
A creative mind can now think none...

I was ready to give you your time....
Just tell me once, what is my crime...
My pride says she asked to be left alone...
Why can't I just become an emotionless drone...
Only if I turn my heart to a stone....
Maybe a different way I would've grown...

You changed all in me do you realise...
Seeing you ignore me increases this pain more than
thrice...
After years today is the day, I cried...
Today once again someone crushed my pride...
But I love you and I'll still give my try...
No matter how much hurt, no matter how much I cry...

It's because I know that even you are hurt...
But it's no way of treating someone as dirt...
I don't know how do I express...
You were a stress reliever but now my biggest stress...
I cannot stop this feeling because you are all that
matters....
Your words hit my heart and my heart shatters...

Your pain you could've shared....
I always showed you that for you I cared...
I got stressed when you were in tension....
Everyone I love has hurt me; did I mention...??
You are hurting me a lot...
A humble request from me, please stop...
Nowadays my heartbeat takes a drop...
You were my priority, you always stood on the top...

I can't stop myself from writing how I feel....
On my feelings I need to set a seal...
Once you waited for me but now for your friends...
I don't want this but maybe this is where it ends....
Just why can't you understand...
You are all I know only thing in life I thought was
grand...

At least you could have turned and looked back....
Only thing I can see in me is a huge crack....
There is no end this...
I hope I am something that she'd miss...
What you are to me cannot be expressed in words...
Everything in front of me, my vision just blurs...

28. Ignorance

It's unknown deep down...
Unknown out there...
Smile and quit the frown...
Our presence is just mere...

Set aside your ignorance...
Gather the knowledge that's scattered...
Our sorrows have no importance...
Our lives have never mattered...

29.

Made of nothing but fire...
With a stone-cold heart....
Death is all that I desire...
While I break apart...
I believe in God's plan...
They are disastrous for my life...
Towards hell I ran...
While stab myself with a knife...

30. Incomplete

Complete disaster...
Incomplete soul...
Just me give a reason to not end this life the whole...

Complete strength...
Incomplete heart...
Everything I do and don't just drift me apart...

Complete fear...
Incomplete mind...
I am the only thing that I cannot find...

31. Inferior

What is it to be an inferior...??
It's the feeling of not being good enough...
The feeling of never escaping the barrier...
The feeling of always being in cuff...

To follow in your footsteps all along...
Don't know how much longer can I stay...
This constant feeling being of wrong...
Carrying this burden throughout the way...

32.

Just finish this even I want to die...
Why kill me every day when you can just say good
bye....
I won't say anything to God, just a hi...
Wish I had wings, far away I'd fly....

There is no room for apologies...
From beneath I shall freeze...
You can never feel what I feel in this breeze...
I am broken but I'll keep going with every piece...

33. Keep Laughing

Laugh on what you dream...
Laugh and don't you scream...
Laugh on the life you've had...
Laugh every time you get sad...
Laugh on the gathered crowd...
Laugh, laugh, LAUGH aloud...

Laugh if the heart still beats...
Laugh on all your defeats...
Laugh in the dead of night...
Laugh while death in sight...
Laugh to the world's end...
Laugh, laugh and just pretend...

34. Maybe

Maybe I'll just slit my wrist...
Cause I can no longer take these taunts...
Maybe I'll just go away in the midst...
Cause your words they haunt...

I would die than hold a regret...
For death is destined...
These words of yours I'll never forget...
My end was predetermined...

35. My Cry

Cry for me o clouds...
Thunder crackling and the pouring sounds...
Cry it out loud and loud....
Sob with me, as we vowed...

Soak them all in my vain...
Pour down my wrath and my pain....
As I flood and never drain....
Drown each of them over & over again...

36. Mother

A crying and kicking new born...
Just went silent in her arm...
Not a sense, but the child knows her...
That's a mother's charm...

She was far too thrilled, when you started to crawl...
Then again, when you first spoke...
And she scolded you on your first brawl...
Then again on your first smoke...

The purest form of love...
That God did ever make...
She has always been the angel from above...
The one that didn't let you break...

When times were hard, she rejoiced by seeing you
grow...
How you'd walk and fall and walk...
Then you grew up, she waited but you didn't show...
But she still stood as your rock...

I'm grateful that you were always by my side...
Your pain and sorrow, from your mother you cannot
hide...
In my life you played the God's hand...

And Mom, I'm afraid of the inevitable...
I need you to escape the inescapable...
Mom, I need more time with you...

Just to say that "I Love You"...

37. Oh, My Dear Self

My dear soul...
Oh, my dear soul I apologize...
Not my fault we both have been others' device...
Try helping!!! Not a good advice...
Hold together maybe the time will get nice...
Maybe till that day we'll become wise...
Oh, my dear soul, hurting you was never my goal...

My dear pride...
Oh, my dear pride I know you are shattered...
I know your pieces are scattered...
But you stand strong, by that I am flattered...
Oh, my dear pride, you no longer need to hide...

My dear mind...
Oh, my dear mind I know these thoughts are killing...
I understand, the body does feel the chilling...
I know there's nothing like healing...
Oh, my dear mind I'm glad you stay kind...

My dear heart
Oh, my dear heart I know we are crushed ...
If only these feelings could be flushed...
If only you were made of stone...
If only I were a drone...
We wouldn't have felt the harshness in the sweet tone...
Things faced quite a few times but still unknown...
Oh, my dear heart people say it's the life's part...

My dear body...
Oh, my dear body you have to bear...
This pain, I know it isn't fair...
I do for all but for me none care...
Through pain and sorrow, ocean to the sky, I stare...
Oh, my dear body please stay erect, with you is going to
be nobody...

Dear myself
Oh, dear myself I'm proud that you survived it all...
You never show but to Lord you made a call...
He didn't answer but you've got to stay tall...
We together fly only and only to fall...
Wish to finish this misery...
Wish God heard my hymnary...
Oh, dear myself to live you've got to survive it
yourself...

38. No More

My life and I, both are waste...
No reason to stay alive...
My sanity is being chased...
Tonight, to hell I drive...
I'll jump from above the cloud...
Cause I've been shattered to my core...
Today I say it aloud...
I don't want to live anymore...

39. My Mind

Day and night I burn...
I bury myself alive...
Next morning I return...
Back to what I strive...

My pen writes what's on my mind...
I give words to what I feel...
This pain shall not make me blind...
But to whom shall I reveal...?

The one I love, too wears a mask...
To whom? Again, I ask...

40. A Truth

There's a warmth I feel...
Suddenly a chaos to unravel...
Just a moment to heal...
Through hell my thoughts travel...

You become my only hope...
In this abyss of holy mess...
I keep hanging to this rope...
As it's the Devil I address...

41. Beauty of Nature

Everything has a story to say...
Stay quiet, listen to the air...
Hold on and see the light ray...
It shows things you can't even bare...

Calm and still is this sea...
Disastrous a few times...
Nature's true beauty is in this tree...
Shadows us irrelevant of our crimes...

42. New Year's

Another New Year...
Another blank book...
Just a desire to disappear...
No matter where I look...

For some a fresh start...
For me, nothing new...
Same pain in the heart...
For some a healing too...

43.

So many New Year's...
Every year a light of hope...
Nothing matters when you are in tears,
Just hanging by that rope...

It's a repeat of same events...
With just a different date...
These years bring heavy presents...
Death shall be our fate...

44.

Another year, in and out,
Nothing yet makes sense...
War and war it's all about,
With them, and own penance...

Hours to Days, Days to Weeks...
Persistent ache yet no one speaks...

The better and worst, already gone...
A numbness lies ahead...
Look up, there will be no dawn...
'Happy New Year' is just to be said...

45. None

No one sees my view...
No one cares about the flaming winds that blew...
Is there anyone who'll understand me as God drew...
Can't survive this, alive in me is only a few...
All the good I do in trash they threw...
One mistake and my hidden feelings they grew...
Help me these feelings from beneath they chew....

For a few days, it felt like everything was falling
together....
Who knew that people would crush the feather....
It's so damn hard to live under this weather....
Yet I tried to stay strong...
Each time I was the one who was held wrong...
Show me a place that I belong...
One last wish, to my death please sing me a song...

46. I Will

People change but the memories don't...
Time goes by but the feelings won't...
Thought I wasn't alone anymore...
Wouldn't let myself fall again that's what I swore...
This time I'll be the one who will soar...
Wait for it even I'll roar...

47. Phantom

Better days yet to come...
I'm filled with only rage...
Been chasing this phantom...
Been trying to break the cage...

Just trying to get a hold...
While I can still see it...
Chilling sensation, can't take the cold...
So, I step back and I quit...

48. Poison

For you are my antidote...
To this life of poison rain...
To the thoughts of slitting throat...
To this insanity I cannot explain...

This page and pen are just a phantom...
The one that you fall for...
The truth behind the sanctum...
This toxin has reached the core...

My silence is the waging war...
Where this poison is my friend...
The poison can never kill my pain...
Cause this agony has no end...

49. Keep Trying

Pride says enough heart says another try...
No matter you are hurt, no matter you cry...
You ignored me still I come back...
Just for you I've already gotten off my track...

Why cannot the ones I love stay....
Am I just a game to play...
Start takes long but the end is in a day...
For which sins of mine do I pay...

50. The Seasons

Frigid I sit without a thought,
Amidst freezing winter breeze...
Was there something I sought,
For this pain to ease...

Gathering courage, I walk out,
With this joyous spring as my guide...
Every breath, a rising doubt,
And every step, I collide...

Waters vaporize, land burns,
Also, my heart in this scorching sun...
Heat waves hit, summer returns,
I have forgotten what is fun...

Sweet scent of monsoon rain,
The heaven weeps and so do I...
Dark black clouds filled with pain,
A melancholy we cry...

Sun rises with the fall,
Shed leaves left to decay...
From somewhere my name they call,
And like the colours this season, I fade away...

51. Flow

I have so much say...
Too much to reveal...
I speak everyday...
But I never heal...

I want to empty my brain...
Let you all know...
Let my thoughts be a rain...
And let it all flow...

52. Soul of the Wanderer

Once upon a time, in a cold dark night...
Within the silence of the mist, and an aching fright...
The soul of a wanderer searching for that light...
Only echoes of sorrow and nothing in sight...

With every step, a haunting presence stalk...
Hemming and hawing, trying to talk...
The wandering soul, rushes to evade...
But wherever he goes, the presence walks...

The poor soul runs through the forest blind...
But the presence that can't be left behind...
At the end of the road when the sun shined...
The bounded presence was only kind...

53. The Ocean

Stand before the ocean...
Hear the whisper of waves...
Flood your sorrow and emotion...
Imitate as it behaves...

The joyful steady current...
The unknown, dark below...
Be alone, if different...
And be your only foe...

Secrets at the bottom...
And scary with the depth...
A friend, no problem...
Ready to drown you every breath...

54. The One

To the one above...
To the one below...
Where is the love...?
Who is my foe...?

The one in my place...
Or the one waiting...
Will you catch up to my pace...?
Or will you just keep hating...?

55. The Unknown

In the world of lies...
In the midst of night...
When the demons rise...
A silhouette searches the light...

For a while he stopped...
Heard someone walk...
In fear he dropped...
Could no longer talk...
Looked towards the Unknown...
With the blood red eyes...
He was never alone...
Realized in the sound of cries...

56. Urge

To let go or to not...
Fight this undying urge...
An unfortunate to the plot...
Through urge shall I emerge...

This state of uncertainty...
This emptiness of thought...
I am down on my knee...
Shall I let go or not...!?

57. Pace

What has happened to me...
World is blur I cannot see...
Everything's running in a blink...
And I can't even think...
Maybe this pain and the world has got a link...

58. Withstand

A bright smile on my face...
The sun shines up high...
A sweet smell in the air...
In the green ocean I lie...

Then comes the cold breeze, and
I find myself in a known unknown...
Repeating the question "Why?"...
And hear myself whisper...
"Your end is nigh"...

This is my day and the torture I withstand...

59. Yes

Yes, I am filled with flaws...
Yes, in everything I crash...
Yes, these are fake claws...
Yes, I am nothing but trash...

Yes, I need someone by my side...
Yes, weak is what I've grown...
Yes, a part of me has died...
Yes, I am afraid to be alone...

60. Not a Puppet

You can't force me I am not your puppet...
I'm just trapped in this net...
I've cried a thousand times but my eyes never got wet...
One day he will kill me on that I can bet...

It's eating me from beneath...
I'm suffocating. Please help me breath...
I've hidden emotions underneath....
I'm just the other one's sheath...

61. Her

Heaven behind her eyes...
Hell behind mine...
It's an art of disguise...
To be hurt and still be fine...

A sweet melody in her voice...
Cry of sorrow in my silence...
I was never her choice...
Neither was mine of this violence...

62.

Today I saw you after so long...
Unbelievably gorgeous you are...
Your eyes they sing a song...
Your sweet voice it's bizarre...
To this planet you don't belong...
Your smile, on my heart a scar...

63.

A glow in her eyes,
It warms me from within...
The sweetest of voice,
That's where I begin...
The joy on her face,
And my problems I forget...
The purest of smile,
My Heaven and my regret...

64. Birth

A world full of wonders...
The topmost is birth...
Within the roaring thunder...
There's a sweet cry on Earth...

The start of a journey...
A journey unknown...
Through anger and agony...
Towards the delightful throne...

Your sorrows and tears...
Are just thorns on the road...
It all disappears...
Once you let it unload...

65.

A cold dark night...
Loud cries of a new soul...
His hold so tight...
So small, the whole...

That was the start,
Of a long and treacherous road...
A distant past,
When a little smile glowed...

66.

Is it supposed to be special, one's birthday...
For since the day you are born, the Reaper lures...
And what is one but a needle in the stacks of hay...
And one never lives, of that, the world ensures...

A journey unknown but a known destination...
Birth and Death the only constant...
Born crying and one lives in agitation...
To live is your penance for Hell is absent...

67.

You entered the world with cries...
The first sound you ever made...
Tiny hands and round eyes...
And lived decade after decade...

A fortune you came to these grounds...
A phenomenon that happened today...
In this life, you shall know no bounds...
Whilst I wish you Happy Birthday...!!!

68. A Guide

I never needed a guide...
Just wanted someone to stand by my side...
There's a lot I have tried...
Immense that I hide...

69. Embrace

All I know is that this pain I shall embrace...
Why shouldn't I when it's the only thing that hit the
pace...
Against who am I fighting in the race...
No name, no body or no face...

70. My Cage

I am a prisoner in my minds cage, someone please help
me out...
Don't want to but I control my rage; no one hears that I
shout...
There's so much I want to but cannot explain about...
I'm lost because I have no destiny, even if I'm on the
right route...

71. Words

Don't know what am I trying...
Can't figure out why...
Just keep myself denying...
Even though I want to cry...

My thoughts are unspoken...
My screams never heard...
Can't they see someone's broken?
Even while it's shown with every word...

72. A Reason

Give me a reason to carry on...
Cannot keep going with broken wings...
Everyone is lost or gone...
Waiting for what my fate brings...

Tired of this nightmare...
I can no more hope...
Leaving this darkness, I don't dare...
But I sliding this slope...

73. My Parts

A part in me screams...
A part in me dead...
A part in me dreams...
A part holding on the thread...

A part in me sore...
A part in me ashamed...
A part cannot take it anymore...
The whole of me is drained...

74. The Pharoah

The King has fallen on his knees...
They are frightened of what awaits...
I smell their fear in this breeze...
Waiting for death at the gates...

Have faith and stand together...
A voice came from the shadow...
All in blood, in hand a feather...
Saying "Bury them with the Pharoah" ...

75. Let it go

I question the other me...
No, I take a pause...
I ask "How broken can we be?"
He replies "Everything happens for a cause..."

"So do we have no value?"
"I know not, but why do you ask?"
"You always stand tall; I ask it for you..."
"Don't care for me, like others just wear a mask..."

"How can I when you and I are the same?"
"I asked that, yet they play their game...

I too get hurt when they leave me out...
But I cannot show..."
"Nevertheless, I hear you scream and shout...
Maybe just let it go..."

76. Spark

Things will surely go downhill...
Calm yourself and stand still...
Take a breath and just observe...
Give a look at every curve...

Move along the path that's dark...
Spread the light because you are the spark...
If you can't, then accept your defeat...
Or gather the courage and face that heat...

About The Author

The Author, here, ME, had nothing to do, except for a start-up to run, bills to pay, game cravings to satisfy, sleep schedule to fix and a life to live, so in utter confusion he started penning down words, and after a cumulative effort of over 1500 days, or what felt like a lifetime, this is all he has to show for it.

Hujefa Vohra, Co-Founder at BeFriends-HAZHTeq Innovations Pvt Ltd started, what can now be called a journey, way back in 2015-16. A kid from 9th grade got too excited when his teacher taught him about rhyme schemes.

Since then, till this date, Hujefa has been trying to write all his thoughts. And even though it took so long for his first book to be, do not think it was a onetime wonder.

Writer's Pocket

Writer's Pocket is a publication house established in 2016. We began with the aim of providing a better publishing platform for aspiring writers and budding poets.

The publishing industry in India (and around the world, to a great extent) is always something of a mystery even to the writers themselves. We are working on making publishing more accessible to everyone.

So far, we have helped over 3,000 writers turn their dreams into reality by publishing the books and continue to do so. By doing so, we also provide some of the best content by Indian writers to the readers.

Want to read more books? Scan this QR code with your smartphone and check out all our books on Amazon.